THE *Alchemy* OF WORDS

# THE Alchemy OF WORDS

Poems of Truth to Transform
Your Inner Landscape

## MENA TEIJEIRO

iUniverse®

# THE ALCHEMY OF WORDS
## POEMS OF TRUTH TO TRANSFORM YOUR INNER LANDSCAPE

iUniverse books may be ordered through booksellers or by contacting:

iUniverse
1663 Liberty Drive
Bloomington, IN 47403
www.iuniverse.com
1-800-Authors (1-800-288-4677)

ISBN: 978-1-5320-3142-7 (sc)
ISBN: 978-1-5320-3141-0 (hc)
ISBN: 978-1-5320-3163-2 (e)

Library of Congress Control Number: 2017913211

Print information available on the last page.

iUniverse rev. date: 09/29/2017

Take a journey of love and surrender
to tickle your soul and awaken your senses.

Remember that which you always are:
Pure. Love. Undefined.

*The Alchemy of Words*
is an invitation for you to allow divine blessings
into your heart and unwrap your sacred gifts.

To my inner child, thank you for your
delightful joy and innocence.

To my higher self, thank you for guiding me with your wisdom.

To all those unexpected teachers with whom I suffered,
thank you for making me run to the treasure within.

To all the healers and friends who held me
so that I could be whole again.

To my family for always being there.

To Source, and the magic of oneness.

I love you.
I *am* you.

Where your treasure is, there also will be your heart.
—Paulo Coelho, *The Alchemist*

# Contents

# Introduction

It's too dark to see, so relax, close your eyes, and follow my voice.

Just behind the gate, the beach expands like a cool and welcoming carpet as I arrive unannounced. Butterflies of excitement appear inside my belly.

The ocean is rippling at the edge, playfully caressing the sand. The ocean and the sand seem to be offering seaweed to each other.

The sky brings me to my knees as I look up to the infinite expanse. Sparkling stars and communities of constellations are painted above me. I invite the heavens to tickle me with their brush.

The crickets sing to the rhythm of the night, and the water plays along with delight. They both seduce me to dance along.

The trees bring messages from Mother. Earth is always supporting me. Yes, I will listen some more.

I bow down in gratitude for this gift of life. I receive the blessings and skip my way home, excited to share my experience with you.

# PART I

# Opportunities

# Sacred Gifts

Divine light
Brought me down
To a land of confusion,
Distress, and illusion.

Lost in the shadows
Of forgotten truth,
I scrambled through
Each moment,

Gripping and searching
With my rambling mind,
In the past and
In the future,

Yet I was always held
In this precious breath
Of allowance and awareness
With love and purity.

So now I dance,
This light that I am
Humbled and strengthened,
Surrendered and grateful.

Shedding the chains
And guided by my heart,
I unwrap the sacred gifts
And share with you this love.

# Rise and Shine

Wake up, sweet children. It's a new day.

New beginnings! What adventure shall we go on today?!
Take in a deep breath. Mm.

Fill your heart with love.
Fill your body with goodness.

Exhale everything that no longer serves you.
Relax. Here, you are safe, loved.

Feel your way through the day.
Let your emotions flow with awareness.

Let the light inspire you.
Let the darkness invite you to open up and cleanse.

And if you stumble, suspend yourself right there.
Look up to the heavens! Look down to earth.

Ask for help.
Ask for guidance.

Ask for ease and grace
For this world is ours to cherish.

We've just learned wrong ways.
We've just forgotten.

We are remembering, sweet children.
Let's bring purity and joy back so we can play.

Receive the gift that you are.
Claim it. Be it.

Ready to rise and shine?!

# In This Moment

In the depth of nothing
Stirs the possibility
Of everything.

In the breath of now
Exists the power
Of the universe.

In the acceptance of life
Continues the flow
Of the divine.

In the grounding of the self
Lies the truth
Of oneness.

# Spell

Morning broke
The spell
Of the night.

No excuses
Are needed
On the new day,

For the past
Is gone,
And today remains

To be lived,
Breathed, and
Braved again.

Wake up!

# Activated

The vortex of change
Has been activated,
And the escape button
Has been destroyed.

Carry on, warrior!
Journey on to the core,
Where silence showers you
With peace and wisdom.

# Alchemy

As I hold my mind in a resting space,
The magic channels through.
Suspended in each moment,
The whispers from another realm
Carry through with love to you.

I do not know where it comes from,
Yet I do know that it is pure and blessed.
A chance to be one with the mystery,
Embraced every night and day,
Carries me with love to you.

# My Wish

My greatest desire is to be
An expression of pure love.

When we claim it soul powerfully,
We bring heaven down to earth.

To remember and know
That through sweet surrender

We become the one
We've been waiting for.

To walk on this earth,
Healing her with each breath.

To become sovereign
And royal in our commands,

Inviting all that is sacred
To join us in this dance,

Creating prosperity,
Love, and light for all.

That is my wish,
And I share it with you.

# Divine Formula

Shine like the sun waking up and
stretching out into the infinite horizon.

Drop the weight,
the stress,
the drama,
the shields,
the struggle.

Let go of the past.
Let go of the future.

Breathe in the light.
Breathe out limitations.

Reclaim your divine existence.
Giggle your sparkly joy without restraint.

Be the *love* that you are so purely.
As I hold you in my heart so dearly,

I choose *you*.
I *am* you.

# Her Secret

Her secret is so juicy and alive
That you might
Want to chase her,
If only for a little while,

To roll in the waves of flow,
And to be tickled by the vibes
Of that child of light,
Fresh out of the tunnel.

Her secret

Is what you already know.
You've just forgotten!

# PART II

# Transformation

# Golden Goddess

"I'm on fire!"
Said the girl
Scarred with flames,
Courageous in her fight.

As the heat burnt through
To expose her soul,
She emerged transformed—            a goddess,
Shining her light of gold.

"I'm on fire!"
Said the woman
Covered in flames,
Ready to take flight.

# Disarming

The walls are crumbling,
Tired of holding themselves
In isolation and struggle.

The rain pours down,
And the water floods
The cracks of uncertainty.

The winds are curious
And find their way
Through each opportunity.

The moon beams steadily,
Lighting up the darkness
And casting shadows of mystery.

And I sit here
Grateful and tired,
Putting my sword down.

# Choosing Love

Streaming tears
Of nothing,
Just illusion tainting
My vision.

I choke and sob
For the lost joy
And the dust
That embittered my taste.

In this now, I ask for
Deep clearing,
As I choose
The light of love.

# Vessel

Oh the human experience...
Even when there is more clarity,
We are not above it.
We're still a part of it.

The more love and compassion we attain,
The more power and awareness we are gifted.
Yet the control is no longer there.
The agenda drops, and we flow from a space,

Beyond the mind,
Beyond needing,
Beyond judgment,

To peace and joy!
For all that arises
Is perfectly in sync
With the next unraveling.

Humility and surrender,
Awe and wonder,
Are the kings and queens,
The magicians of each moment.

I bow to the light.
I accept to be
A vessel for thee.

# Surrender

Choking
At the very bottom
With a grip on my life.

Do I fight
And keep struggling
In the mud of yesterday?

Or do I melt, surrendering
Into the field of light,
Where a new canvas is waiting?

Sadness and joy are a breath away.
As I allow the tears to flow,
The opening of my heart grows.

And I hold myself where I am:
Love and light
In this now.

# Open to Receive

Take a walk to
The other side
Of the rainbow.

Take a look to
See beyond
The apparent reality.

Take a breath to
Still yourself
And find clarity.

Take a moment to
Thank yourself
For all that you do.

Why?
Because I love you.

# Fresh Start

At the end
Of the journey,
There is nothing
To prove,

For we are
Always
That
Which I am,

Dancing to
This song
Of eternal
Joy and bliss,

Being
In the now
Of play and
Divine flow.

So, do I go deep into
This cosmic
Party of
Transformation,

Or do I stay and resist,
And complain,
And suffer,

The pain

Of illusion?
Such confusion!
I let go
And am renewed.

It is always the end.
And I begin
Afresh
On this new inspired day.

# Contrast

It is in the darkness that we desire the light.
It is in the sunshine that we beg for shade.
It is in forgetting that we shield ourselves from our pain.
It is in loving that we begin again;

To live the life we deserve to breathe.
To be the one we enjoy to be.
Contrast is the teacher;
Love, the ultimate preacher.

You, me, we,
One again.
Won today.

# Collapsing

Fragments of polarity
Painted as positive or negative,

Distracting our life from
The purity of expression.

Time to say goodbye, shattered self,
Collapsing into the ocean of oneness.

I am forever free and
Endlessly alive!

# Beyond the Zone

I am the Divine in disguise,
Waiting for you to find me
In the ray of light,

For the shadow cast upon you
Is simply a breath away
From the blessed garden.

Step outside your comfort zone
To be stripped of the cobwebs
And stand raw in the thunder of truth.

# Lightning

A line crossed my mind.
It was the damp sensation
Of a misconstrued thought.

The repeating storms of life.
In strife, I pondered my options,
And anxiety took hold of my peace.

By grace, I was hit by lightning,
The kind that wakes you into clarity,
And the shadows of the past dissolve,

Leaving way for a clear pasture
Where the heart can roam free
And the wings stretch out with delight.

# What Am I?

I *am* that space of everything that allows you
To paint the masterpiece of your dreams.

I *am* the space of possibility
Where you can *be* your heart's desire.

I *am* here. There. In you. Without you.
Him. Her. Your child. Your lover. Your mother.
Your brother. The stranger. And the other.

I *am* it all.
I *am* the breath.
I *am* the *fire*.
I *am* that I *am* in truth.

Unchanging.
Enabling.
Supporting.
Guiding.
Inviting.

I *am* the experience,
The experiencer,
The cosmic dancer,

That which remembers what was once forgotten,
That which loves where hate lived,
That which forgives what once was rejected,

That which sings after it was muted,
That which creates where destruction once ruled,
That which contemplates where it was judged.

The womb of creation,
The black hole of existence.
Twirling galaxies of magical dust
Dancing in sync with the life within.

Endless. Rest here...
For it is all there is.

# I Am

"What are you?" asks the reflection.

I can't say.
What I do know is what I'm not:

Not this body,
Not my thoughts,
Not even what you think I am.
I'm not that.

Oh! Wait… YES.

I am love.

# Undefined

I *am* undefined,
Free,

Beyond judgment,
Detached from right or wrong,

Light and dark,
Boundless and beyond definition,

Acknowledging the shades of life,
Experiencing each moment,

Aware of my savory emotions,
Surrendering them to Source.

Even when I stand naked in Truth,
The highs and the lows

Are just an integral part
Of this human adventure,

For we are all one
On this journey of exploration.

Embracing the shadows with our heart,
The path floods and *all* is light.

# Surrender Again

I surrender my mind
To higher wisdom.

I surrender my doing
To inspired action.

I surrender my body
To my crystalline structure.

I surrender this moment
To the joy of being.

I surrender my ego
To the humility of grace.

I surrender my life
To the one I *am*.

# Fields of Gold

Love is the altar of life,
And what overflows from it
Is the abundance
Of creation.

When things and work
Become our masters,
We enslave ourselves,
Depleting our true riches.

So follow that blazing heart
Into the fire of now.
Then, the fields of gold
Will appear.

# True Life

Deep, deep within our soul
Is the key to transformation,

Allowing us to believe and to know
That all answers we already hold.

The *we* is the issue
We must first resolve,

For 'who' or 'what' makes it
Possible for us to evolve.

When we understand,
When our hearts are aligned,

Then we end the journey.
Alas, a new humankind!

Life has begun again,
This time true.

Oh, I am very grateful.
Yes. You can be too.

# The Mystery

So we live among the blind
And breathe out wisdom,
Guided by our hearts
And the humility of service.

We are one, and yet the puzzle
Pieces are awkward at best
And awakening is far for most
In the predawn of earth.

Light bewitches
The shadows of duality
To unravel the mystery
Of being love.

# Dying to Live

Where is the joy that blossomed in my heart?
Where is the passion that fueled my mornings?
Where is the compassion that held you in the light?
Where is the spirit that opened doors to other universes?
Where is the hunger for truth and the thirst for flow?

Dying

In this torment of deep emotions and flooding dreams,
In the false hopes of yesterday and the insignificant cheers of disappearing friends,
In the pitless hole of disappointment and the bleeding soul betrayed by illusion,
In the deafening silence of indifference.

Vanished into the desert of lack,
Burning in the ashes of the unforgiving fire,
Scattered by the winds of change,
And dampened by the incessant tides.

Buried forever
Into the womb of the mother,
And then her love and warmth
Sprouts these seeds,

Rebirthing
Deeper love,
Bubbling joy,

Burning passion,
Bold truth,
Sensual flow,
Sweet compassion.

And we see that all the struggles were
Moments of transformation.
The discomfort of growth
Was well worth the

Glory of being.

# The Breath of Death

Death is coming
to this known life,
as I can no longer
take another
stagnant breath.

Death is welcome,
as I know life
has a lighter rhythm
and another,
richer breath.

Death is home,
when I know life
as a long letting go
for another
blessed breath.

To fully live,
we die to untruth.
With that sovereign breath
we are reborn—
free.

# The Mountain

I feel wild like a rugged mountain…

That has stood firm through hurricanes,
Taken a deep breath through floods,

Held the fire within during dark days,
Crumbled with the earthquakes, and

Shed tears with the melting icecaps
And raging thunderstorms,

To then erupt with passion
And birth higher grounds,

Holding space for new life
And promising beginnings.

# *Flame*

While heaven rains down blessings,
Earth nurtures our essence.

Still we complain of loss and confusion,
Disconnected from our source.

Focused on a derailed world,
Not knowing what we're worth,

We blame them!
We blame him.
We blame someone over there…

Flame! *Flame*
Is the better word.
Focus on the flame within.

Then we will win
The universe of love.

# Fear Not

We are afraid to show our pain,
Thinking we will be rejected.

We are afraid to share our struggles,
Believing we will lose our capacity to inspire.

We are afraid to truly love another,
Believing something will be taken away from us.

We are afraid to feel weakness,
Thinking we will be trampled upon.

We are afraid to let go and cry,
Believing it to be a useless experience.

In fact, it is our raw imperfections
That make us lovable and approachable.

It is the absence of fear
That makes us truly *live*.

So, I vow to face all fears
And embrace my humanity.

# Balcony

Silence can hear,
Feel, and know what
Noise and distraction
Will never comprehend.

Enjoying the bliss of home
And the winding journey
To the ever present
Space within.

Crickets and cars,
Stars and lights,
Vibrant on this stage.
All divine in this Now.

# Infection

Innocence was slashed
Into an infected wound,
And the hope of tomorrow
Became the disgust of betrayal.

Seduced by the dark
Corners of isolation,
She withered away
Into a ball of abandonment.

Falling down the cliff
Of inspired heights,
She whispered one last
Plea for *help*!

The universe heard clearly
That cry from this child of life,
And swooped down
With a loving hand,

Giving way to warmth
And to a spark of clarity
That snapped her back
Into the breath of Now.

Empowered in this present,
She shook off the shadows
And spread her wings
To take flight.

# PART III

## Love

# *Love Is*

Waking up with awe and gratitude
Even when the alarm is piercing.

Smelling the fragrant roses
Through the fertilizer.

Smiling with twinkling eyes
When others still don't get you.

Gently purring out each exhalation
When there's only you to hold.

Being kissed by the setting sun
When the boat has sailed away,

And caressed by the evening breeze
When you've lost your sweater.

Going to sleep, snuggled and held
When the bed is cold.

Trusting all is good
When all is raw.

Love is
The fabric of life.
Return to love
And it fully blossoms.

Love is…

Waking up with awe and gratitude
As you feel your sweetheart

Smelling the fragrant roses
That you picked just yesterday,

Smiling with twinkling eyes
As you dive into the depth of the soul,

Gently purring out each exhalation
As you relax into the now,

Being kissed by the setting sun
After a day of joy and adventure,

Being caressed by the evening breeze
With tickles and laughter,

Going to sleep snuggled and held,
Surrendering to the moment, and

Trusting that all is good,
Because it is.

# Evolving Love

Distant love,
Your silence would have shattered me
Had I not already been broken
Into nakedness, unarmed.

Changing love,
You whispered of your love to me,
And yet as soon as the winds shifted,
You cast it away like old leaves.

Infant love,
You forgot what you had felt in the summer
During that cold winter day
Without vision of the blossoming spring.

Doubtful love,
Your past betrayed the future,
As the present was denied its breath.
It quickly plummeted to its death in agony.

Impulsive love,
Your fire burned bright and seduced
All ladybugs to come near to your flame of passion,
Leaving ashes in the hearts of your victims.

Careless love,
You made me feel like a queen,
But then you placed me on the buffet,
Surrounded by the other appetizers.

Divine love,
You came to me at the end of my suffering,
Radiant and inspired, peaceful and steady,
Letting me know it was all worth it.

# Holding You

I hold you in my heart
With the strength of a black hole.

I hold you in my dreams
With the sweet knowing that you are real.

I hold you in my breath
With the certainty that I'll never forget the next inhale.

I hold you in my mind
With the clarity of a perfect formula.

I hold you in my body
With an electric current flowing.

I hold you in my hand
With a big smile on my lips.

Why?

When I hold me, we are one,
So I will hold you forever.

# The Bird

A singing bird landed
As I opened the window
To my soul.

It chanted of life,
Of love, and then of joy
And possibilities.

I smiled from
My heart
And knew

That as its nest
I could
Inspire it to fly.

Then we could
Both soar
Into the horizon.

# The Rose

That dawn, the rose felt chilly,
Yet the warmth of the stem
Was proof of her aliveness.

As the sun majestically appeared,
The rose recognized him immediately
And welcomed another day.

Steady and consistent,
Radiant and ever so present,
He advanced higher into the sky,

Hence inviting the rose to
Relax with the warmth of the rays
And gently unfold each delicate petal.

The rose became the fragrant one
Generously sharing her beauty
In the garden around her.

As the shadows started to dance
And the light got dimmer,
She wrapped herself again.

Yet the rose was not the same,
For the love of the sun
Allowed her to remember her own grace.

# The Sun's Memoir

Beloved withering rose,
I remember your heightened glory,
As I was present for your unraveling.

You shared with me your essence,
And I burned my fire of passion,
Only to see it extinguished the next moment.

Now I remember what was then,
And I cherish this vivid memory,
To nourish the blossoms of the future.

# Heart's Longing

If I were to share
The extent of my love,
Your heart would expand
To a space of surrender:

The void in the womb of earth;
The promise of heaven;
The breath of the newborn;
The gift of another day.

If I were to share
The extent of my love,
Your heart would remember
My longing for you.

# Core Truth

If you stopped for a few
Moments to listen to my vibes,
I would tell you the secrets
Of this unfolding universe,

Wrap you with the flow of grace
So you could fly into the wild embrace of mystery
That is waiting for you at the corner
Of here and now

To expand your horizons
Beyond worry and concern,
From problems that don't really exist
And petty desires that can't satisfy your soul.

Then you would remember
These whispers that I murmur
As memories of never-ending knowing.
Truth, behold, the core is blinding

Love.

# Rising in Love

I have fallen in love
Several times in this life,
And in that stumble I
Gave away my power.

Now I rise in love
And share what I am
As I fly free above
The old paradigm.

Meet me high above
The drama of humanity
To embody oneness
In flesh and blood.

Now we can dance
To the rhythm of harmony,
Embracing life and experiencing
The joy of being love.

# Ask and Be Ready

Ask for love;
Be ready to crack open.

Ask for peace;
Be ready to communicate with humility.

Ask for compassion;
Be ready to understand the child within.

Ask for truth;
Be ready to face your shadows.

Ask for joy;
Be ready to skip, giggle, and cuddle.

Ask for surrender;
Be ready to let go of the grip.

Ask for grace;
Be ready to receive magnificence.

Ask for aliveness;
Be ready to explore.

Go!

# Commitment

Come here, my darling.
Rest now with me.
You are so precious.

Come here, my queen.
Rest now with joy.
You are sovereign.

Come here, my inspiration.
Rest now with delight.
You are so creative.

Come here, my breath.
Rest now as you exhale.
You are very present.

You know what happened next?

"Marry me," said my soul.
"Then I can give you
Your heart's desires."

And I did.
I *do*.

# Merging

When I visit you
In that sacred space
Where time stands still,

I feel you in my breath,
I know you in my heart,
I hold you in my soul.

You disarm into love,
And I am that I am,
So we get lost

In the flow of oneness,
Dissolving polarity and
Unifying souls.

# Nectar of Life

I wanted to hold you
In my nurturing chest,
Swaying you with the currents
And the tides beneath the full moon.

My heart yearned to be
Burning like a sacred fire
The truth of its passion,
Yet you were never mine.

So my love grew and grew,
Unexpressed and bursting
Through the cracks,
Until there no longer was a *me*.

Now I am the nectar of life
Running through your veins,
Breathing you into life, and
Kissing your lips into smiles.

# Ecstasy

I am full
Of nothing,
Which desires
Not.

I am void
of drama
And alive in
Stillness.

I am soul
In the form
Of one
More human.

I am that,
Not what
I have thought
To be.

I am now,
In a space
Of not knowing,
Yet trusting.

*I am, I am*
The flow
Of love
In ecstasy.

# Letting You Know

What can I say,
What can I do,
What can I sing,
What can I bring,

To let you know
That I love you?

What can I believe,
What can I let go,
What can I change,
What can I create,

To let you know
I'm ready for you?

What can I suggest,
What can I plan,
What can I consider,
What can I share,

To let you know
You're a part of me?

What I can be,
What I can receive,
What I can surrender,
What I can hold within,

Lets you know
I *am* here for you.

# Stranger Love

I see you as if you were a stranger,
Yet I know you intimately.

There's a newness each time
I look into the depths of your eyes.

Awe and expansive curiosity
Flame this moment of connection.

# Inspire Me

What you say is
Irrelevant without aligned actions.

What you aspire to
Is an ego trap if you are trying to prove something.

What you hold above you (other than Source)
Is how you give your power away.

What you promise is
Uncertain if you leave it for the future.

What you withhold from love
Is an act of treason.

What you do not attempt is
A lost opportunity.

It's *how* you live that inspires me,

With
Courage and truth,
Passion and consistency,
Connection and compassion,
Surrender and wisdom,
Remembering that the journey *is* it,

With an undying conviction that right *here* is all we need.

Love in each other's presence,
Love within,
Love without.

# Unleashed

What if I could find a space to *be*?

Give freely and peacefully breathe with my whole body.
Move effortlessly without being accused of provoking.
Share my dreams without being anchored by doubts.

What if I could be seen in this moment of truth
Beyond that which is apparent, and from your heart
Without being a target of attachment?

What if your simple presence
Invited me to dissolve the barriers to my soul
and permitted me to blossom into the one I *am*?

What if you could *be* with me, without hurry,
free of expectations and with no agenda?

Well, then, I would be unleashed!

# Dreams of Truth

My soul is singing
A dream of a life that is
Within.

It's here, so dear to me,
Beloved existence!
I smile within and then without,

For I don't have a doubt
That what we cherish,
We bring about.

# Ignited

You ignited a passion
That flamed straight
To my soul,

A fire so pure
That I could not
Have imagined

The power of love
Awakens a strong
Current,

And your eyes,
with that smile,
Say it's true.

# Those Eyes

Behind the dark glasses
You guarded your treasure,
And as you unveiled,
I melted into your eyes.

In awe of their gentle power
And of their sweet confidence,
I wandered toward your soul
And opened my heart to yours.

Strangers in a land of knowing,
Flowing with the love of *one*,
Waiting and breathing,
Each moment closer.

# Embodied Love

I stand, and in the space that I hold for us,
A wave of joy rushes in.
You have wanted to appear
For a long, long time.

You step forth confidently
Upon my field
With the certainty of someone
Who desires it with all his heart.

And I recognize you before
Your presence is fully made,
Because I have dreamt of you
During eternal moments.

I smile with your knowing smile.
A flash of lightning strikes within us,
The light of grace, the truth of God,
Embodied in our embrace.

# PART IV

# Disappointment

# Confusion

Sadness dilutes the
Core of my existence.

What's the point of love
That can't be shared?

What's the goal of life
If passion is watered down?

What's the truth of my heart
If it is denied its expression?

What *is* it all for?

# Giving Up to Source

Deep into these feelings I go,
    defeated,
        for I no longer care for this life of
            *misery.*
Always back to aloneness and suffering.

    I give to you this life.
    Do what you *will.*

# Fueled

Wrestling with my discomfort,
I growl at the emotions that
Keep me a prisoner in no-man's-land.

Angry and sad, alone and confused.
Restless days and nights
Fuel me, urging me to break
Free.

# Children

For years you were

The torment of coming back home,
The needle that pricked my heart,
And the tears that burnt my eyes.

With your tantrums and complaints,
You saddened my mornings
And fogged my playful nature.

I tried and tried, and then I felt
Exhausted from the futile efforts,
So I found refuge alone inside.

Away in my cave of nurturing light,
I healed my pains, and now
I am love and free to guide you.

# River of Tears

The times of sorrow are looming.
I no longer know if I have
The strength to smile again,

For the tears in my eyes
Claim their turn to be the protagonist,
To be seen, to be felt, to be wept

into the ocean of oneness.

# Just Be

When I am crying,
Let my tears form rivers of clearing.

When I am angry,
Let my rage burn into passion.

When I am sad,
Let me call out for help.

When I am confused,
Let me be okay with not knowing.

When I am giving up,
Let me surrender to the higher path.

When I am exhausted,
Let me fall into the peace of the beloved.

When I am excited,
Let me sow the seeds of creation.

When I am,
Let me just be.

# Projection

In the silence of the night
At the end of the day,

The apparent aloneness
Is just a screenplay,

For all that we know,
And all that we feel,

Is the light of the
One that we are.

# False Intentions

I saw a glimpse
of the man
you could be.

You felt seen and
loved, and
yet you faltered,

For your ego
inflated and
took flight,

to fall lower
into the waters
of ambition,

tainted with
insecurity, greed,
and false intentions.

# Rising Beyond

The light turned on bright
And I danced to the flow of life,
Twirling in the grace of now.

Guiding and loving,
Knowing and feeling,
Trusting and surrendering.

The envy turned on bright
As her ego got trampled,
Twisting her sense of superiority.

Learning and growing,
Understanding and allowing,
Choosing and letting go

Of that space of jealousy
And rising beyond it
To a sacred temple,

I am free to be.

# Obstructions

Your heart loved me,
Yet your fears
Got in your heart's way.

Your soul knew me,
Yet your ego
Got in our way.

Your eyes saw me,
Yet your confusion
Got in the way.

I forgive you,
For you live not
In your truth.

# Love It All

Endless moments before
Truly knowing
We are the one,

Our heightened senses
Vividly perceive all
Drama and pain.

Life generously gives us
Multiple logical reasons
To isolate ourselves and be alone.

Alas, we are hit by one too many,
So we victoriously choose to
Love it all.

# PART V

# Support

# Angel

If I were an angel,
I would fly just above you
Each day, each night,

Guard you from your fears,
Whisper words of comfort,
Hold your heart in mine.

I would take you on a journey
To the ends of this earth,
Right to the edge,

Where rules are just dances
Of flow and surrender,
No right or wrong.

Where delightful laughter from
Invincible masters
Tickles the senses,

Where the fruit of life
Is delicious, and melting
Into the womb of Source,

To spring back forth
With power and elation,
To tell you again and again,

"I love you!"

If I were an angel,
I'd sit here next to you,
Humming this song.

# Death Becomes Him

An angel by my side,

So soft and gentle,
So loving and kind.

A memory of a friend
Who reached out to me.

Now all he wants to do
Is to be of service.

Yes, he's your ally for
What you desire.

Just trust and admire.

# The Bird

I am the bird that flies to the horizon
And realizes that there is no destination.

I am the bird that flies away
And realizes that home is always with me.

I am the bird that flies in a flock
And realizes the grace of togetherness.

I am the bird that flies freely
And realizes that life is an exciting adventure.

I am the bird that flies and swoops
And realizes that change is inevitable.

I am the bird that flies and rests
And realizes its love for the nest.

# I Got You

Fall back into this moment.
We've rushed ahead into the future.

Fall back into trust.
We've forgotten that all this is a gift.

Fall back into play.
We've forgotten this is our playground.

Fall back into forgiveness.
We've forgotten how to let go and grow.

Fall back into love.
We've forgotten we are one.

Fall back into nothing.
We've forgotten we are everything.

Fall back into the night.
We've forgotten it will carry us to a new beginning.

Fall back.
I got you.

# Injustice

Rage broke through
And became tears of
Disbelief,

For the pain
They endured
Was not right.

And the light
That I am
Knows

There's another
Way for
Us all.

So I rolled up
My sleeves
Of action,

And spilled
My love
With passion,

Overflowing
My gifts
To the world.

# Unconditional Love

So I choose to be
Like the pink rose,
Unconditional in my love,

Fragrant and fresh,
Blossoming and opening up
To the light,

Fearless and more
Courageous than
Before.

Mm…
Smell that rose.

Let it grow.
Let it show
Me how.

# Waiting

Oh, how patiently
You wait for me,
Unhurried
And quiet,

Singing your song
And carrying
Your tune
In silence,

Inviting me
At every moment
To show up
And twirl.

I give
Thanks for your
Presence
Divine flow.

# Home Here

The search ends
When we find
We are home.

Here with our
      fire,
      passions,
      patience,
      compassion,
      deep love,
      courage,
      transparency.

Here with our
      fumbles,
      sadness,
      doubts,
      anger,
      despair,
      indecision,
      contempt.

Here with our best friend,
Our own internal voice
Of endless support and self-love,
Who is less than a breath away
And who allows the light and blessings
To shower upon us.

Here I can
        hold myself,
        laugh,
        cry with my pain,
        celebrate my laughter,
        burn in the fire,
        listen to my inner child,
        die, and be reborn.

Here I am whole to be
Everything my soul desires.

I am free to share
With whom I dare,

To open my heart,
To create and delight,
To shine so free.

So be
Here.

# Play Now with Me

Suspended in this moment,
    No past,
    No future,
        Simply *here*.

The past can hold us in usual patterns repeating endlessly,
Keeping us trapped in our small definitions of life.

The future can create anxiety and a
Sense of not having arrived yet.

The answer is in *play*.
Feel the joy that comes when you know that everything is taken
care of,

That life is unraveling to support you.
Receive the abundance!

In that presence, let life move us into aligned *action*,
Moved from a deep wisdom.

Stillness is *not* doing nothing.
It's the absence of both rejection and attachment,

While flowing with what *is* present at each moment.
Be *here* so intensely that it's all there *is*.

# Clarity

When all else fails...

There's God,
The universe,
Consciousness,
The Creator.

As we surrender...

The limitations fall,
The doing becomes being,
The heartache becomes heart expansion,
The shadows become the dancer.

When all else fails...

That itself becomes the joke,
For in trusting we find

We've always been adored,
We've always had everything we needed,
We've always had the key to heaven on earth.

There was no aloneness.
There was no lack.
There was no key.

Just you and me,
A bit confused.

Now we can see.
Now we can be
Love to thee.

# Sleep

Change is the constant in my life.
Love is the inspiration in my life.
Friendship is the laughter in my life.
Family is the gratitude in my life.
Sleep is the refuge in my life.

Good night…

# Simplicity

The experience of being present with what arises…

Here. Not in the mind.
Here. In the heart.
Here. With the one we are.

In the simplicity of being,

We heal,
We create,
We share in love.

# My Son

It's not what you do,
Not what you think or say,
Not anyone's opinion,
That ultimately matters.

Simply give your best
At each moment
From your heart
In service to humanity.

Without agenda,
Without needing to prove
Or show others who you are
Or what you deserve.

For you are always
The son of the Creator,
A spark of cosmic dust,
An experience of the universe.

Simply shed the dirt
And the blinds from truth
So you can unravel into
A life of joy and creation.

Love, loved, loving,
You are
Now.

# Get Ready

8 – Breathe.

7 – Relax.

6 – Ground into the Earth.

5 – Receive higher perspectives.

4 – Sense the sun in my grateful heart.

3 – Flow like the ocean.

2 – Spread my wings like a bird.

1 – Be love in action.

Ready for adventure!

# It's Time

Ticktock,
The clock goes.
Yet it's always
Now.

The time
Of truth,
To be and
Fly free.

Ticktock,
The awake grow
Wiser and bolder
Now.

# Time for Coffee

I would sleep a thousand years
To hide away from my heartbreak,
For its acid sensation burns through
To the scars of my soul.

As I hibernate away in the cave of winter,
The blossoms wither away and
The sun can't shine upon
My raw and wounded nakedness.

Frozen heartbeat and crystallized tears
Form the landscape of this now;
So, I find refuge in this cup
Of hot, sweet, and enlivening coffee.

# Ask

Let go and fall
into this precious moment,
Which is more vibrant than the past, and
more powerful than our future, and
Is so full of goodness.

Trust it.
Breathe it.
Remove the barriers.
Stop defending.

For in our peace and self-love,
the aggression dissolves and
the blessings arrive.

Ask for the most amazing life.
Ask for ease and grace.

Listen to your heart's desire.
Don't give up.... Faith is required, along with
determination and persistence.

We *arrive* (where we always were)
when we start dancing with this flow.

Then our hearts light up with
the innocence of laughter and joy.
                    Sensual dance.
                        Tingly giggles.
                            Expansive energy.
                                Belly breaths.
                                    Beating heart.

Ask and you shall receive
what you need.

# Stillness

Stillness is a friend
Who listens unconditionally.

Stillness is a partner
Who supports unconditionally.

Stillness is a mother
Who loves unconditionally.

Stillness is a father
Who guides unconditionally.

Stillness is a stranger
Who smiles unconditionally.

Stillness is an angel
Who hovers unconditionally.

Stillness is a full moon
That shines unconditionally.

Stillness is the truth,
Which *is*.

# PART VI

# Inspired Breaths

Experience is the mother of wisdom.
Curiosity is the father of knowledge.
Presence is the child of an intense life.

•——•

Open so many doors
That the walls collapse
And *oneness* prevails.

•——•

Love is the passion to share the now
So profoundly that it is all there is.

•——•

Let it go…
And if you need to
Hold on to something,
Catch a rainbow!

•——•

The journey is eternal,
So stop looking
For the destination.
The glory of life
Awakens endlessly
As the present.

•——•

I see you!
Beyond the appearance,
Beyond the ignorance,
Beyond the origin,

I see you.
I know you.
I *am* you.

For love, courage, and truth
Are the fabric of divine existence.

●——●

Hold life as you hold the moon—
In awe!

●——●

Open up your bubbling heart and
Let it beat to the rhythm of life.

●——●

Listen to your heart,
Even if it's whispering
Something unexpected.

●——●

When I let go of *who* I am,
I find that I am
Love.

●——●

In the silence of presence,
Everything is heard, held, and loved.

●——●

We're always
In the right place

At the right time
When we're here.
Then…
Lightning strikes.

In that honoring of the moment,
You are, you breathe, and you know
All there is.

Wake up.
Yes, you!

Eyes wide open,
Heart expanded,
Grounded firmly,
Aiming toward the light,
Walls collapsing,
Mind calming down,
Surrendered to flow.

Truth, behold this morning glory!

To wake up and have the capacity to see
With fresh eyes the same view,
Which is completely different…

Wake up, wake up, wake up!

Time to breathe.
Time to dance.

Time to smile.
Time to be.
Time to hug.
Time to listen.
Time to surrender
To the day
      As
        It
           Unfolds with the awe and
*Wonder*
        Of
        A child!

➤——➤

Sunrise paints a picture.
No frame can contain
The magic it evokes!

➤——➤

Each end is a new beginning,
And this evening is a celebration
Of the journey of the past,
The excitement for the future,
And the gratitude of this moment.

➤——➤

Mesmerized,
The mind dissolves
Into the awe of the heart.

➤——➤

Crack
      And there's no going
*Back,*

For what          is done
        is past
And only now
Remains as the          *space*
Where truth can unravel.

➤——➤

Sometimes we find
That there is nothing lost.
All we have to do is be
Present to this now.

➤——➤

I shed my tears unguarded.
They carry such deep sorrow
That they could carve out
The eternal pain of humankind
And reach the core of love.

➤——➤

Life is the masterpiece
Of existence.

We make of it
What we dare to unfold.

Brave ones,
Awaken.

➤——➤

When the heart is ready to see,
Life shows up in full bloom.

➤——➤

I look out at the sky with
The same eyes of yesterday,
Yet today they are fresh
With the awe of now.

➤——➤

What if we always remembered
We are the light?
Dare to try!

➤——➤

I see the horizon,
Yet my soul
Just wants to
Rest here and now.

Dynamic rest is
A surrendered flow
That carries us
In the womb of grace.

➤——➤

When we starve the ego of success,
Victory belongs to the self
And the whole earth blossoms.

➤——➤

Cherish your single moments,
For soon you will be embraced
Soul True that you shall abide
In the eternal bliss of one

Understanding, passionate,
And ever expanding love.

❯——❯

As I create you within me,
You are.
As you create me within you,
I am.

Time is a mere disguise
For what *is*.
Self-discovery opens the portal
To love.

❯——❯

Time melted the lush garden
Into the essence of love,
And the full splendor of the blossoming
Transformed the decay into gratitude.

❯——❯

LOL friends.
Love. Only love.

❯——❯

I feel trapped in the cocoon
Of my transformation,

Crumpled into a ball of nothing,
Ready to explode in this now,

And I expand my wings of freedom
To be the one I love.

⮕

As a smile curves along my lips,
I savor a deep and long exhale
And a tingling in my heart—
The gifts we overlook
Until we discover them.

⮕

I lost my mind and found the one
Love within that doesn't label or judge,
A serene space of being,
Dancing within and without
For balanced presence.

⮕

*Love* used to be a verb.
Now it's a statement of truth.

It *is* what I am,
What you are.

It's the fabric of consciousness.

⮕

The mermaid came from
The ocean of oneness
With her unexpected innocence

And sparkling aura
To be and play in the flow.

May life caress your soul
With the warmth of butterfly tickles,
Awakening your inner child
To an ecstasy that rips you wide open,
To a love that is unending,
And overflows into pure creation.

Be like the fragrant flower,
That offers its nectar
To the flow of life.

# Who Am I?

Me

Mena
Menafesting
The truth of the self.

Eternal love
Blossoming
Into a fulfilled life.

Me

Mena
Amen

www.menafesting.com

Printed in the United States
By Bookmasters